THE CONGREGATIONAL
RESPONSE
TO CLERGY BETRAYALS OF TRUST

A Liturgical Press Book

THE CONGREGATIONAL RESPONSE TO CLERGY BETRAYALS OF TRUST

Nancy Myer Hopkins

Published
in association with the
Interfaith Sexual Trauma Institute
Collegeville, Minnesota

THE LITURGICAL PRESS
Collegeville, Minnesota

Designed by Frank Kacmarcik, OBL.S.B.

Library of Congress Cataloging-in-Publication Data

Hopkins, Nancy Myer.
    The congregational response to clergy betrayals of trust / Nancy
Myer Hopkins.
        p.   cm.
    "Published in association with the Interfaith Sexual Trauma
Institute, Collegeville, Minnesota."
    Includes bibliographical references.
    ISBN 0-8146-2441-3 (alk. paper)
    1. Sexual misconduct by clergy.   2. Reconciliation—Religious
aspects—Christianity.   3. Trust.   4. Clergy—Professional ethics.
5. Sexual abuse victims—Pastoral counseling of.   I. Interfaith
Sexual Trauma Institute (Collegeville, Minn.)   II. Title.
BV4392.5.H66   1998
253—dc21   97-44854
                                                                        CIP

CONTENTS

FOREWORD

We welcome this volume that is sponsored by the Interfaith Sexual Trauma Institute. The Institute was created in May 1994 by St. John's Abbey and University in partnership with the ISTI Board to address issues within ministry of sexual abuse, exploitation, and harassment through research, education, and publication. The vision of ISTI is the building of healthy, safe, and trustworthy communities of faith.

In its statement of purpose for the Institute, the ISTI Board, with membership from some fifteen Jewish and Christian traditions, strongly affirms the goodness of human sexuality and advocates respectful relationship through the appropriate use of power within communities of all religious traditions. Everyone stands to gain by examining openly together whatever we discover are the issues and by providing the means to confidently promote an informed awareness of our common failure. We must look critically at history, sexuality, human relationships, and our collective struggle to develop sexual meaning.

ISTI believes that human sexuality is sacred; misuse of power underlies all forms of sexual compromise, compromise that violates human dignity and harms individuals and communities both emotionally and spiritually. Healing and restoration are possible for survivors, offenders, and their communities through a complex and painful process. However, truth telling and justice making are integral to change and healing in individuals and institutions.

THE GOALS OF ISTI ARE TO

1 encourage understanding of sexual misconduct through interdisciplinary seminars, conferences, and seminary instruction;

2 develop models of intervention, psychological and spiritual healing, restitution, and recovery of community trust in collaboration with such persons as victims, offenders, religious leaders, and those in the helping professions;

3 support the systematic study of and theological reflection on healthy human sexuality and appropriate use of power;

4 publish materials regarding victims and healing, offenders and rehabilitation, and spiritual communities and their transformation;

5 advance research on sexual abuse, exploitation, harassment, and their prevention;

6 collect and disseminate accurate information about issues of sexual misconduct;

7 network with other professional organizations and agencies that deal with issues of sexual misconduct.

We welcome suggestions. For information on treatment programs, newsletters, workshops and seminars, and other resources for victims and offenders, contact:

Interfaith Sexual Trauma Institute (ISTI)
St. John's Abbey and University Collegeville, MN 56321

Phone: 320-363-3994 Fax: 320-363-3954

E-mail: isti@csbsju.edu
Internet: http://www.osb.org/isti/

The Congregational Response

INTRODUCTION

Your congregation is currently facing clergy sexual misconduct or a major trust betrayal on the part of a leader. No matter when these events happened, you are just now hearing about them, and chances are that you are experiencing confusion and anger, even chaos. A lot of people have responded differently, perhaps depending on how close they were to the clergyperson or how believable they think the allegations are.

No matter how far in the past the events were, if they were covered up it is not unusual for people to be troubled and unable to work together very well. In some cases congregations can be plagued by serious conflict or depressed for years as a direct result of misconduct. This is especially so if a congregation has not had a chance to know what the charges are and to work together to recover.

When a minister or priest or other spiritual leader betrays the trust, people are seriously affected. This is because we expect our clergy to be trustworthy with our children and safe for all of us when we bring our vulnerabilities to God through them and the Church. When that trust is shattered, the feelings of betrayal can be overwhelming. Not everyone will respond the same way, but all can be said to be going through a grieving process in response to profound losses. This booklet is offered to help you understand many of the reasons misconduct is so troubling. It should help explain how people will react differently and often be in conflict with each other. We have worked through enough of these cases so that we can tell you many of the predictable responses and give some helpful strategies for dealing with them. In this way you will have a good chance of moving through the pain and emerging a stronger and much-renewed congregation.

1

WHAT ARE WE TALKING ABOUT?

First, some definitions: *Sexual misconduct* includes child abuse and also sexual harassment or exploitation of adult parishioners. *Child abuse* is defined by all states as abuse of minors or impaired adults (developmentally delayed, mentally ill, unconscious). It is a reportable offense, and church officials will always defer to the state for immediate action, applying the church's discipline afterwards.

Sexual harassment is primarily understood to occur between a church leader and a person in his employ, a colleague, or one being mentored by him. Included in harassment are sexualized conversations and innuendo, establishment of a hostile climate for women, unwelcome touching and hugging, pressure for dates, excluding women from meetings, sabotaging women's work, sexist jokes, hostile put-downs, public humiliation, exaggerated or mocking "courtesy," obscene or harassing phone calls, discussion of one's partner's sexual inadequacies, "accidentally" brushing sexual parts of the body, pressing or rubbing up against the victim, "full body hugs," erotic kissing, leaning over or otherwise invading another's space, sexual "sneak attacks," soliciting sexual services, stalking, sexual assault. I give such a complete list here as a way of helping people understand the scope of harassing behaviors.[1]

[1] Katherine A. Mackinnon, *Backoff!: How to Confront and Stop Sexual Harassment and Harassers* (New York: Simon & Schuster, 1993).

Harassment has the effect of reducing a woman to her sexual function. It is demeaning and is used to intimidate. If a person feels that she is being harassed and asks the harasser to stop, and if he sincerely apologizes and stops, then the behavior might have genuinely been an honest mistake. However, this seldom happens. Usually the harasser minimizes the behavior, claims that the person is over sensitive, escalates the behavior, or in severe cases, initiates reprisals upon being reported. This subsequent behavior is to be understood as a continuation of the original harassment and is as good an indication as any that true harassment was happening in the first place. I am using the male pronoun exclusively when speaking of harassment because the perpetrator is nearly always a male. Harassment is largely driven by the cultural imbalance between male and female in our society and is particularly damaging when it coincides with another kind of power.

Sexual exploitation of adult members of a congregation can include everything listed above as harassment, but there is often another dimension, which continues to be confusing to many. Harassment is understood right from the start as constituting *unwanted* sexual advances. Exploitation, on the other hand, often involves a vulnerable congregant who initially might have felt confused or ambivalent about the advances. This would be especially so if that person had been "set up" over a period of time by the cleric and told he or she was "special" and desperately needed, thus becoming flattered by the attention and desirous of the contact. Occasionally those who are exploited will have been actively seeking the sexual contact and initiating it, often reliving their experience as previous victims of incest and consequently vulnerable to revictimization. It is often not until later that the damage done by the relationship becomes apparent to the person who has been harmed by it. Because of the power that resides in the role of the ordained, which will be spelled out more clearly below, the responsibility for maintaining the boundaries *always* rests with the ordained person.

Many have asked, "But what about those many generations of clerics who often chose a mate from the congregation, not only with the Church's blessing but with the families of prospective brides encouraging them?" The sexual revolution has intervened, meaning that most younger adults have probably long been sexually active outside the marriage covenant. Realistically, this also includes clergy, who are finding vocations to ordination later in life. Also, we now understand much more fully the power residing in the clerical role, which renders a vulnerable congregant unable to truly give consent to such a relationship.

Clergy dating of a congregant continues to be a controversial issue, with most writers saying to single clergy who may want to date an eligible congregant, "Don't even think about it."[2] However, some are saying that clergy naturally relate to congregants in a dual role more than do other professionals. If single clergy wish to explore a relationship with the intent of finding a life partner, the greatest likelihood of finding a compatible partner who shares the same values might be right in the congregation. This can create a huge dilemma.

[2] See Marie Fortune, *Is Nothing Sacred? When Sex Invades the Pastoral Relationship* (New York: Harper & Row, 1989); Marilyn Peterson, *At Person Risk: Boundary Violations in Professional-Client Relationships* (New York: W. W. Norton, 1992); and Peter Rutter, *Sex in the Forbidden Zone* (Los Angeles: Jeremy Tarcher, 1989).

By exploring what a nonabusive relationship between a cleric and a parishioner might look like, we can see that the cases that wind up as potential lawsuits do not resemble a respectful and mutual relationship at all. According to Lebacqz and Barton, *all* of the following safeguards must be in place for the exploration of a mutual and committed relationship between cleric and parishioner: (1) Both are eligible. (2) The parishioner attends another congregation, at least temporarily, and gets another pastor. (3) The cleric's superiors know he or she is dating a congregant, and they are providing regular supervision for that cleric's entire pastoral ministry. (4) The congregant has not been in counseling with the cleric, or currently undergoing a major life transition, or grieving. (5) The relationship does not have to be a secret. Even with all these conditions in place to ensure that mutual consent is possible, the authors caution that this is still a very risky enterprise.[3]

It is also possible for clergy to abuse power in ways that are not particularly sexual. *Frequent outbursts of temper and constantly putting people down* seem to be particularly problematic. This is when the behavior exists in extreme form, which is sometimes hard to distinguish from normal, run-of-the-mill kinds of behavior. We are talking here about a matter of duration and degree. This usually does not become clear unless congregants are willing to compare notes and document the behavior over time and then present the documentation to church officials. In the past church officials have often identified such behavior as just a manifestation of conflict and have brought in conflict

[3] Karen Lebacqz and Ronald Barton, *Sex in the Parish* (Louisville, Ky.: Westminster/John Knox, 1991).

consultants to deal with it, operating on the assumption that everyone is on a level playing field. But the same principle applies here as with other abuses of power. The clergy are responsible for not abusing the power of their position to intimidate and terrorize congregants. In some cases, discipline may be called for, not conflict resolution.

What complicates this situation is that there can also be laypeople in a congregation who have varying degrees of secular power attributable to such things as possession of wealth, or position, or tied to age, race, class, or gender. If there are laypersons who are also willing to abuse their secular power in a congregation and if they get into conflict with a cleric, it can be very hard to sort out the players and the varieties of power that are being abused. For instance, a young woman cleric in conflict with an older very wealthy male who is willing to sexually harass her is probably one down in the power equation. All cases have to be seen as unique with so many variables to be considered.

Misuse or theft of funds are also examples of power abuse that can be very damaging. Trust levels fall, and many people are directly affected. In fact, all those who have contributed to the church are harmed. Because money continues to be as taboo a subject in church circles as sex, many of the same principles of congregational intervention apply.

If a cleric is severely impaired because of *substance abuse,* this can also create a troubled congregation. The dynamics are similar to alcoholic families, and therefore strategies of intervention that work with alcoholic families will often work when a cleric is intervened on. One or two educational sessions will not be enough, however. Congregations are far more complex than families, and people will often bring their own unresolved family-of-origin issues into such congregations, perhaps even finding themselves comfortable there because there is a replication of one's own alcoholic system. Much hard work is indicated to help move as many as are willing toward recovery.

Now, a word about terminology. When charges are made but the truth of the charges are neither proved nor disproved, we speak of the *complainants* and the *accused.* When charges have been proved, we speak of the *survivor* and the *offender.* The term "survivor" is appropriate for someone who was a victim but who has started on the road to recovery by coming forward.

2

WHAT ARE THE ORIGINS OF POWER IN THE CLERICAL ROLE?

Clergy have sacred power attached to their role, and much of that power is unconsciously given and received. Over the centuries the church has, wittingly or unwittingly, enhanced that power. Power, in and of itself, is not a bad thing. Most clergy are aware that they possess it, and they treat it as the gift it is: from God and the Church. A healthy clergyperson will be well aware of the seductiveness of that power and sit somewhat uneasily with it. Early in his ministry, Jesus wrestled in the wilderness with the possibilities of his own power (Matt 4:1-11). Every clergyperson who is striving to be faithful to his or her calling will have wrestled in the wilderness—some, many times over.

But a small fraction will abuse that power. Ironically, often the more self-aware ones will recognize later that they did not feel at all powerful at the time. A common pattern of clergy who violate sexual boundaries is that they have violated other boundaries first. They can get into a downward spiral of overwork, laboring under the illusion that only they can minister effectively to this congregation. This is sometimes called a "savior fantasy." Then, when they are in the process of crashing, their own unmet needs overwhelm them and they feel entitled to some relief. This is when many are most at risk to step over the line.

3

THE PROFESSIONAL HELPER

Clergy have some role power in common with other helping professionals. Doctors, teachers, and therapists, as well as clergy, experience *transference*. Transference happens when we bring our unresolved issues with former authority figures into our relationships with current authority figures. Because clergy are often seen as parental figures, we sometimes view them as surrogate parents. In some denominations, this is encouraged by the use of titles such as "Father." If our relationship with our parents was largely positive, we will naturally be disposed to view our clergy favorably. If parental relationships were troubled, however, then we may transfer some of our negative feelings into the relationship with our clergy. It is possible to become aware of what is happening if we pay attention to our inner lives and continue to work directly with our own parents to settle any unresolved issues we may have.

If a clergyperson does not understand the dynamics of transference, he or she is much more at risk to violate boundaries. This is especially true when adults transfer the wound of incest or other serious abuse into the pastoral relationship. On the surface this can look like an attempt at seduction. It is not unusual for a person who is acting seductively with a care-giver to desire sexual contact at the moment, being totally out of touch with his or her unconscious process. However, a clergyperson who recognizes what is going on will not fall into the trap of acting on feelings of arousal generated by *countertransference*. Countertransference has a variety of manifestations, but the one most relevant to this discussion is that the feelings brought into the relationship by the congregant can be mirrored in the clergyperson.

Projection. Simply put, this is the "pedestal phenomenon." This is a natural and normal process, which we all do to some extent. It is only when projection reaches unhealthy levels or when those receiving projections begin to take them seriously that projection becomes a problem. Projections can be either positive or negative. Hero worship is an example of positive projection. Sports figures and other public people get a lot of projection, much of it harmless. If we see in admired people qualities we wish we had ourselves, we often are projecting. The difficulty comes if we do not work to actually make those qualities our own. When we take responsibility for ourselves, we reduce the degree to which we project. With our clergy, if we expect them to be holy for us so we do not have to continuously develop our own spiritual lives or never have any faults, then projection can take on unhealthy aspects.

There is a trap here for clergy as well. Receiving a lot of positive projections can feel awfully good. It takes a constant reality check to be aware that projection may be in play. Some comments from congregants that may signal positive projection are, "Father, you're so wonderful!" (especially if uttered early in the relationship when there has not been enough personal contact to bear this out) or, "You will have to (a) pray, (b) bless us with your presence, (c) work your magic, or (d) keep us on the straight and narrow." On the other hand, voiced appreciation for specific actions taken or things said are more likely to be genuine expressions of regard rather than the result of positive projection run amok.

Projection can also be negative. Sometimes the people who are most prone to doing positive projection can easily switch to negative projection. When we project those parts of ourselves that we are uncomfortable about onto others, much harm can be done. Again, the key to reducing the extent of negative projection each one of us does is to be willing to take a fearless self-inventory and even list the traits of the person who has "gotten under our skin." Do those traits somehow also describe ourselves? In order for any criticism of clergy to be constructive, the communication must be delivered directly and the specific behavior, along with the effects of that behavior, described.

Projection, when it is positive, contributes to sacred power. However, negative projection can be so virulent in some settings that clergy are then more at risk to burn out on the job or betray the trust in some way.

4

THE UNIQUENESS OF THE CLERICAL ROLE

There are other origins of sacred power in addition to those processes clergy have in common with other authority figures. Clergy often embody the divine for people. The priest standing at the altar is an obvious example. Many Protestant clergy vest, use the title "Reverend," sit above the congregation, preach from even higher elevations, and dominate worship with little if any lay participation. Rabbis occupy a powerful role as teacher, with much overlay into other sacred dimensions. The preacher who strides about the stage with well-worn Bible in hand also embodies the divine. Many people have an almost fanatical fear of getting caught swearing in front of a clergyperson. The presence of a clergyperson at the bedside of one who is critically ill is imperative for many. Lay presence, though comforting, does not carry the powerful impact that clergy presence does. For many there seems to be an unspoken expectation that the clergyperson, as a representative of God, can perform a miracle and restore the person to health.

The priest or minister is also involved intimately with major transitions in the lives of parishioners. This involvement creates a major bond, usually of affection. Clergy are probably the only professionals today who are still welcomed and expected in our homes. We often trust clergy with our innermost fears and turn to them during periods of

21

personal crisis. We trust them with our children. When a pastoral trust betrayal is revealed, it can feel like those intense moments of loss or joy—at the time experienced as blessed by our pastor's presence—have been turned to ashes.

In the wake of so many egregious boundary violations that have surfaced recently in virtually all denominations, some are questioning if the institution has contributed to the problem by intensifying the unconscious dynamics in the power differential. Given that a certain unconscious need for a "holy person" is always there, what things intensify or diminish the effects? Can it be possible to teach congregants not to give away so much of their spiritual power to another? Ironically, direct experience with clergy sexual misconduct in a congregation has been shown to accomplish that outcome.[4] But what a traumatic and destructive way this is to learn a very hard lesson!

Small wonder, then, that learning about a pastor's betrayal of trust becomes an extremely traumatizing event in the life of a congregation. However, we know that not being told openly about what has happened and not dealing with the feelings generated together as a community is far more damaging to a congregation.

[4] Stephen Rossetti, "Broken Symbols: Child Sexual Abuse and the Priesthood," *Today's Parish* (September 1992).

5

HOW DO THE VARIOUS TYPES
OF ABUSE AFFECT CONGREGATIONS?

Congregations facing *child abuse* will be extremely trauma-tized on hearing the news but may work toward acceptance faster than if they were dealing with allegations of harass-ment or adult exploitation. This is in large part because in our culture we have finally arrived at the understanding that child abuse is *always* wrong. Even here, however, some people who cannot believe the allegations will question the veracity of the survivor or quickly marginalize the vic-tim(s) if he or she came from a family that can somehow be blamed for letting their child get "in harm's way."

It continues to be very difficult for many people to under-stand how damaging *sexual harassment* is. Because men and women have different gendered experiences of being sexually pursued, the gender gap of understanding still often looks more like a chasm. Women are never flattered by harassment, and can immediately recognize that this be-havior (described above) is in no way to be taken as a strat-egy to indicate a serious and respectful sexual advance. Furthermore, if it is coming from the clergyperson who is supposed to represent the safe and sacred, it can create enormous confusion and self-doubt. Once this behavior has surfaced, the recipient is forever consigned to a course of hypervigilance. The underlying question then becomes, "How far is he likely to go?"

Sexual exploitation is also difficult for many people to understand. Typically a few people are deeply harmed in secret, but many have absolutely no clue that anything is amiss. In fact, a person who is willing to target certain vulnerable individuals may have at the same time "wooed" many others with his or her charm and charisma. This helps explain how hard it is for some to believe that this person could have ever betrayed the trust. The usual excuse offered by the cleric who is charged with exploitation of an adult is that they were consenting adults, so therefore there was no harm done. Hopefully, when more people become educated about the impossibility of mutual consent, more will be empowered to not be exploited. Clergy should learn to monitor their own responses and not fall into the trap of thinking they can get involved with vulnerable congregants with impunity.

Emotional abuse can be more broad-based in its impact, with many more people directly affected. Sometimes this combines with other forms of abuse. It is often much harder to intervene and call this kind of power-abusing cleric to account. As noted above, church officials often make the mistake of defining this as conflict. If such a cleric is removed, the congregational response may be one of immediate relief. However, the damage done can still go underground if it is not directly addressed and a process offered to the congregation for healing.

Theft also causes great trauma. Some common ways I have seen this manifested are stealing from church funds or from congregants, getting written into people's wills, and getting insurance checks. The most egregious is getting power of attorney and the death benefits of a spouse. Another is getting a huge loan from the congregation and reneging on it. In several cases clergy have visited parishioners' homes after release from the hospital and stolen their pain medication. While doing an intervention and imposing discipline is fairly straightforward in these cases, the congregation's response can be very intense and mirror responses to sexual misconduct. Themes in common are the issue of trust betrayal and the general taboo of discussing the topic. It is imperative that a congregation be offered a process for healing.

Substance abuse can create an entire alcoholic system. Much of the learning gleaned from twelve-step programs can be appropriate here. Many people may be presented with an opportunity to explore their own personal and family issues relative to substance abuse. There is no reason why a congregation could not enter recovery together, dealing with the issues raised on many levels.

Please remember that we are still talking about only a small number of clergy who abuse their power. By far the large majority of clergy in all denominations faithfully exercise their ministry. It is easy to lose this perspective when one is in a congregation undergoing a major crisis.

6

OTHER FACTORS THAT INFLUENCE HOW WELL A CONGREGATION WILL RECOVER

The continued presence of those who have been directly harmed

When the aggrieved or their families remain in the congregation, parishioners may take longer to arrive at acceptance, but often recovery for all will be more complete. However, if those who have been directly wounded leave, or even worse, are driven out, and the congregation does not have to face that particular pain, the recovery may be seriously compromised. Those who brought forward complaints are the ones who courageously found their voices and called the church to account. They took tremendous risks to do so. When they remain and are supported to go on their own healing journey, recovery for the entire community will ultimately be deeper and more lasting.

The continued presence of the offender in the wider community and/or persons in the congregation who are fiercely defending him or her

If there is one single factor that impedes congregational healing, this is it. Clergy who have left a congregation in a timely and healthy way know that they must stay away for a good length of time in order to give their successor a chance to get established. If any friendships are maintained, it is common courtesy to refrain from discussing congregational politics. But clergy who have been involuntarily terminated because of an incident of power abuse will often violate these norms continuously, even after having been told that they should have no more contact.

There are many different diagnostic categories of clergy who betray the trust. Perhaps the least problematic from the congregational standpoint is the one-time offender, usually acting out as a result of stress and capable of immediately knowing he or she did something wrong. These people have well-developed consciences and are sometimes called "neurotics," "lovesick," or "wanderers." They will sometimes self-report and will express genuine remorse. Such a person will have enough sense to stay away from the congregation after removal, which is still an appropriate consequence. The potential for him or her to be restored eventually to ministry *in another congregation* is good, but allowing a significant period for recovery is indicated.

Another major diagnostic category is that of the obsessive-compulsive disorder. Sometimes called sexual addiction, addicts will seldom self-report, but if caught and confronted they will often admit that their lives are out of control. Some pedophiles fall into this category. Twelve-step programs and continuous lifelong therapy are indicated. As addicts progress through recovery genuine remorse is possible, and this will lead to the desire to make amends. Some can return to a ministry if never placed with their "target" population. Openness about their history and regular supervision are required to assure continued safety for everyone. At some point reconciliation with direct victims and the congregation may be possible, but those harmed are appropriately the ones to make the overture, and this should not be rushed. Five years into recovery seems to be the bare minimum for such an offender to be ready to face the world with his or her truth.

The most difficult diagnostic category, from the standpoint of the congregation, is the person with a character disorder. A common disorder is narcissism. While the few women who have offended sexually usually fall into the two categories above, the narcissistic offending clergyperson is nearly always a male. This is because narcissism itself often arises as a result of some kind of childhood abuse, and such an injury often results in either an overvaluing or undervaluing of the self. In our culture overvaluing is culturally conditioned for males, undervaluing is culturally conditioned for females. In fact, the female with narcissistic traits can frequently become the target for the male with a similar background of childhood abuse.[5] It sometimes seems as if there are a disproportionate number of narcissists who are attracted to ordination. The opportunity to be center stage and to be in control may have something to do with this. Persons with a character disorder will often set up many in a congregation to accept as normal a wide variety of abuses of power. Some of these abuses will be subtle and not so noticeable at first. A narcissist will put himself at the center of everything, and nothing will happen without his approval. He is often isolated from the wider church and takes the congregation with him into that isolation. If denominational polity permits it, some will be very long-tenured, and create a virtual fiefdom.

[5] James N. Poling, *The Abuse of Power: A Theological Problem* (Nashville: Abingdon, 1991).

Many will be attracted to such a cleric's personality, which is often charming and charismatic. To complicate things even further, the narcissist is often a very effective preacher; he gets things done and is an attentive pastor when people are in crisis. This may be because those who are temporarily in need represent no threat to him. Congregations often grow in numbers with a narcissist at the helm. Many, both men and women, will "fall in love" with the narcissist, who encourages dependency. A small number of those who fall in love will eventually get sexually involved. The most dependent of that number may never see themselves as victims and will continue to fiercely defend the cleric after charges are brought. Another group of people, those who are stronger and therefore a threat, will be emotionally or sexually harassed, even exploited when vulnerable. It is these people who are likely to eventually blow the whistle.

When charges are brought against a clergyperson with a character disorder, the typical response of the one charged is to stonewall, deny, attack the complainants, rally allies in the congregation, and fight the charges, often to the bitter end. This behavior is consistent with all that has gone before, and if anyone had any doubt that the charges were true, this behavior will help convince many who are not enthralled with the cleric's personality. However, there is usually a small but very vocal group who are incapable or unwilling to believe the charges, no matter how well documented they are or how credible the complainants. It is this situation, the seeds of which have been sown long before the crisis, that seems to make it hardest for congregations to recover. A person with a character disorder is so self-centered that he can never really grasp how he might have harmed others. The probability of ever returning to ministry or reconciling with the congregation or those directly harmed is not good.

7

WHAT IS THE EXPERIENCE OF THOSE DIRECTLY HARMED?

Persons harmed by power abuse will not much care which diagnostic category the offender falls into. Their trust has been betrayed by someone they had every right to expect would be safe, and the effects are shattering. This kind of betrayal hits at the very core of a person's ability to believe in God and to trust the self. Victims are sometimes vulnerable in a wide variety of ways, and that is often why they are unconsciously singled out. However, all who are in a pastoral relationship are vulnerable to some extent. Depending on the type and severity of the abuse, the losses range from relatively mild to catastrophic.

It is only necessary to examine how one is robbed of his or her power in these relationships in order to understand that power abuse lies at the heart of all clergy trust betrayals. Often silenced, threatened, thrown into great confusion, or reliving earlier experiences of abuse at the hand of trusted family members, victims suffer enormously. At the same time, there may be some aspects of the relationship they find compelling. This, too, mirrors the experience of incest. When a congregant has been violated by a pastor and used to gratify the pastor's needs, the potential harm cannot be overestimated.

Those who are targets of verbal or sexual harassment or sexual advances that stop short of sexual intercourse have to deal with another set of internal responses. Strong feelings of confusion and self-doubt emerge as a result of this kind of behavior. Did he really mean to do that? Am I overreacting? What might he try next? Can I ever be safe in his presence? Should I report? Maybe I should just leave.

A person who has been harmed by any destructive behavior starts regaining power the moment the decision is made that the behavior is wrong and must be stopped. Often this point does not come without hard individual work and strong support from another person such as a therapist or family member. Coming forward to name the abuse and begin the process of justice-making feels exceedingly risky, but for recovery to begin, it is a vital first step. How the church receives the information can do much to either hinder or help that process of recovery. By church, in this instance, I am referring not only to church officials but also to the congregation.

Once an adjudication has been made and the cleric has been found guilty of some sort of power abuse, congregants will want to guard against revictimization of anyone who made a complaint. The human tendency in these circumstances is to blame the victim. Yet this very human response is entirely inappropriate in a group of people who are striving together to be faithful to God's word. If some members of the congregation are allowed to continue blaming the victim, the effect can be even more traumatizing than the original abuse was.

8

WHY IS DISCLOSURE SO IMPORTANT?

Throughout the following discussion I am assuming that the allegations have been carefully considered and the victims found to be credible, that a judgment has been made in a fair process, and that the allegations have been determined to be true, even if the person accused continues to deny them or to minimize the effects of his or her behavior.

When a clergyperson offends against even one member of his or her congregation, this is abuse within the context of the community that affects the entire church. There are primary issues of safety. Justice-making requires truth telling as the first element. Congregants who are told nothing frequently "know" something terrible happened anyway. Imaginations often run wild, with people thinking things that might be worse than they really are. When congregations are "protected" from the truth by church leaders, they often feel demeaned and patronized. They can be set up for a troubled existence for a very long time.

While disclosure is nearly always desirable, occasionally, it is not possible. If a vulnerable victim is still in the congregation and does not wish to have the case made public because he or she will be easily identifiable, disclosure may not be possible, or it may have to wait. When deciding about disclosure, I usually put the needs of those likely to be affected in the following order: (1) direct victims. (2) the congregation and other secondary victims. (3) the clergyperson, after a determination of guilt has been made.

Often when a case breaks the cleric will be removed immediately, but an investigation will then ensue to determine if the charges are credible. When this happens it throws the congregation into an excruciating limbo that can go on for months. Church officials will be rightly honoring the church's legal process, and in the beginning they may not be able to say very much, if anything. There seems to be a wide difference between denominations on this matter, and even within denominations. If at all possible, a visit from a church official telling what little can be told and why more information is not possible now will help a congregation get through this period. This is similar to a ministry of presence when people are buried in rubble after an explosion and we do not yet know their fate. Many denominations are working to update their disciplinary laws to expedite matters and consider more carefully the direct victim's needs and those of the congregation. Most disciplinary laws were written with the idea that the worst thing a cleric could be charged with would be heresy.

Once it is decided that disclosure can happen, it must be said that not everyone in a congregation will want to hear the truth. In addition, truth telling in the short run creates additional chaos and confusion. However, this period will not last forever if the congregation is offered sensitive and competent assistance in getting through the crisis and the follow-up period. In fact, congregations frequently grow spiritually and emerge stronger than ever if they face the situation together.

9

WHAT CAN WE EXPECT?

Knowing what to expect can do much to help people recover. When the news is first disclosed, people will be in shock. It will be hard to absorb the information, and many will simply not believe it. Many of the emotions experienced will mirror those of the grief process. People will emerge from shock on different timetables and then usually go into a denial or an anger stage. This will largely depend on the personal experience one has had with the clergyperson. Those who may have found their way to that congregation because they were attracted to the personality of the clergyperson, and who have only experienced his or her pastoral presence in a positive way, can find it nearly impossible to believe that this pastor whom they loved so much was capable of doing harm. On the other hand, those who have had some negative experiences, perhaps being aware of a variety of harassing behaviors or even being subjected to them, will have no trouble at all believing the news. Others—those in the middle—will be variously affected, often overcome by intense sadness but able to assume a "wait and see" attitude. They may gradually come to believe that serious harm was done as they experience a good process for bringing them to the point of understanding.

A certain amount of conflict is inevitable between people who are at the extreme ends of believing differently about the situation. This conflict can be made much worse if many of those who are more moderate allow themselves to get embroiled. Recognizing that this is by nature an extremely reactive setting will help lower the general anxiety and prevent things from spinning out of control. The steadying presence of a skilled interim or regular consultant or a denominational official can do much to provide support at this time.

10

THE CRISIS MEETING

The five main components of the congregational healing process we use when adjudication has happened and it becomes possible to share the news with the congregation are (1) truth telling, (2) sharing and the validation of feelings, (3) education, (4) spiritual reflection, (5) answering the question "Where do we go from here?"

The crisis meeting, or meetings, will ideally happen one to two weeks after a letter has been sent out informing people of the situation and inviting them to a meeting. Consultants skilled in doing congregational trauma interventions or people prepared by the tradition to form a pastoral response team will help facilitate the meeting. It is not advisable to have the meeting in the context of regular worship. People all need to know in advance what the meeting is about and to be able to self-select in or out of the process. They should be told the meeting will last for four hours and that they will be expected to stay the whole time.

Truth telling happens first. This should always be done by a church official who is not a member of the congregation. Enough information should be given so that people understand the scope and duration of the abuse and cannot either minimize the behavior or blow it out of proportion in their imaginations. Something of the survivor's experience can be summarized for them, but the survivor will not normally be present, or identified by name. The chronology of how the case was handled is vital information to share, and sometimes the denomination's lawyer can do that part of the disclosure. Time can be given for questions of clarification.

Not everyone will want to do truth telling. However, it is an essential part of the process and cannot be avoided. It is important for a majority of the lay leadership, any clergy remaining on staff, and judicatory officials to all be behind the decision to disclose.

Feelings work comes next. This is done in small groups, using some ground rules to make it as safe as possible for people. People speak until finished about their feelings, not engaging in dialogue until all have had a chance to speak. Facilitators from the congregation trained in advance can make sure these ground rules are observed.

Education follows and will be determined in advance by assessment of what the congregation needs to understand about this particular case.

Spiritual reflection is done in small groups or the larger group by asking people to tell each other where God is for them in this, or what hymn or Bible story they are reminded of, or where their hope lies.

Answering the question "Where do we go from here?" or "What else do you need in order to be able to heal?" is the last task of the meeting. If time is short an immediate thoughtful answer will not be possible, but the point will be made that this is the *beginning* of a recovery process, not the end, and that much more work needs to be done. The intention of the lay leaders to appoint a task force to oversee the continuing healing process for the parish can be announced.

11

THE FOLLOW-UP PERIOD

The task force will be composed of people who attended a crisis meeting and are convinced that there is more healing work to be done. It is neither necessary or desirable to try to get representation from those who continue to insist that the clergyperson is wrongly accused. The task-force group will somehow survey the congregation to assess the continuing needs and then plan ways to address those needs. This will typically consist of offering work for individuals and small groups, and later, follow-up congregational meetings. There can be a wide variety of offerings, such as therapy groups for survivors of childhood abuse, groups to examine one's family of origin, parish based twelve-step groups, groups to explore the congregation's history or to examine issues of sexuality or of violence in the media. A group of men and women could profitably explore gendered experiences together. Spirituality groups in response to trust betrayals of spiritual leaders may be necessary. Eventually the time will come for a healing service. However, we do not recommend that this be done prematurely as a way of getting closure too soon. Some congregations have, however, held ongoing healing services at regular intervals.

The crisis meeting is essentially a trauma debriefing with some added components. This, however, is only the beginning of the healing process. The themes that surface during the first meeting or meetings will be echoed throughout the follow-up period. Many people at the time of the crisis meeting will feel better and say things like "now we are able to get on with our lives." But there are usually some huge hurdles left to get over. Sometimes those most unable to hear the truth will opt out of the congregational crisis meeting. As stated in the discussion of types of diagnostic categories above, an amazing number of clergy who are willing to exploit the power of their office seem to end up living in the community and to be willing to continue abusing the residue of their power. A small but vocal and determined group of "champions" of the accused can do much to threaten the ongoing healing process of the congregation, especially if they continue to occupy center stage in the life of the congregation and everyone is tiptoeing around them.

One issue almost always surfaces at this point. This issue is presented by those in the congregation who considered themselves friends of the clergyperson. They are rightly concerned about him or her as a person who also needs support. Being completely cut off from contact with him or her seems unduly harsh and punitive and lacking in compassion. But if the clergyperson continues to be in total denial despite adjudication that proves him or her guilty, contact is not good for either congregant or cleric. Destructive behavior does have consequences. It is difficult even for those who are not congregants and are carefully chosen and trained to support the offender to stay connected and still encourage accountability.

A major problem with those who are unable to believe the charges is that they usually need to find someone else to blame. Thus the survivor often becomes the primary target, or the anger is focused on denominational officials for their "mishandling" of the situation. If at the same time there are known survivors or family members in the congregation, there can be numerous destructive skirmishes between the two groups and their allies. Survivors, or their family members, can be revictimized in ways that can be even more damaging than the original abuse. Coinciding with this development is the fact that survivors typically tap increasingly into their rage as time goes by. Going through anger and rage is an important part of the healing process for survivors. However, their recovery is greatly impeded if they get stuck there, especially if they are held there by members of the congregation who blame them. We repeat it like a mantra: *Survivors are never to blame.*

One way to address this dynamic is to invite people in small groups to share their positive, negative, or mixed *first-person-only* experiences of the offending cleric's ministry. By listening carefully to one another, people can gradually reach the conclusion that the situation is not quite as simple as it seems and that for many ambivalence, or holding two truths in tension, is the predominant task. When people are able to conclude that their pastor could have done both very helpful and very harmful things, this is a mark of progress. This is *not* to say that the harmful and abusive behavior is to be excused or minimized. Anyone who has offended against the community must be made to face consequences. Indeed, for the offender facing the consequences is often the first step to recovery.

Sharing personal experiences will move many from their previously hardened positions but will probably not greatly impact those who identify with survivors so much that they only want revenge, and those who are completely defended around the idea that the clergyperson could do no harm. Some people in either group may have become so entrenched that they will be unable to hear anything else on the issue.

At some point it will be necessary to move ahead without trying to bring every last person along. Some people will inevitably leave the congregation. This is not necessarily a bad thing, but church people are often disturbed when even one person leaves. If one views this community as one that is getting healthy, however, and that some people are not willing to grow along with the rest, then they have some choices; change and grow, or leave.

12

FORGIVE AND FORGET?

This is one of the most oft-used phrases that leaps to the lips of those who cannot come to grips with a clergyperson's abusive behavior. It is a phrase guaranteed to throw anyone brought up in the church into a state of utter confusion. In the context of clergy abuse, however, forgiveness and reconciliation can never at the outset be a unilateral act. Nor can one person decide when it is appropriate for another to forgive. It is God's prerogative to forgive, and true repentance and a willingness to make amends are stern prerequisites. Furthermore, asking victims to forgive another's act when they are being blamed directly or indirectly for that act is the height of cruelty.

But as people of faith, we must always hold to the eventual possibility of forgiveness and reconciliation. If all parties—those who harmed and those who were harmed—do their own hard work of recovery, true forgiveness can eventually happen. We are talking a matter of years here, not months.

13

UNDERLYING CAUSES

After the crisis period is over, there are many areas of congregational life that will need to be examined in the wake of clerical power abuse. Some of the most common are listed below:

1. What are the cultural and institutional factors that have created a climate in which power can be abused?

The cultural context I am referring to here is middle class and North American. Many of our values seem to favor commercialism, individualism, property rights, and rigidly hierarchical structures in nearly all institutions. In this late twentieth century, more in the United States than in Canada, communal values seem to have taken a back seat, with self-interest being paramount. I have heard it said that we have been transformed from citizens into consumers and tax-payers, pitted against one another in battles of self-interest. This is the cultural context for everything that is going on in the church and other institutions.

Women and children have long been less powerful in this culture. It was not until the early part of this century that laws making them the property of their husbands were struck down. In overwhelming numbers, women and children have been the victims of clergy sexual misconduct. Facing sexual misconduct in the Church is a very counter-cultural thing to do. Those survivors who have courageously found their voices are not only confronting the Church with power abuse but all other forms of oppression are potentially up for challenge. This naturally causes conflict; challenging the status quo always does that.

The Church is indeed the body of Christ, but it is also a very human institution. How do we learn to live with this paradox? It may be that the most important work the Church has to do in this time and place is to face the harsh and painful truths about the institution that have so long been hidden from our view.

2. What cultural and institutional messages do we get about appropriate and healthy sexuality?

Our attitudes toward sexuality can best be described as obsessed and repressed at the same time. The portrayal in the media of sex and violence with racism and sexism embedded in it is a tremendous force for ill. It is defended in the name of "freedom of speech," but is really intended to sell products. A legacy we have from the Church is that when we speak of "morality" we are often limiting that to sexual activity. Sometimes we become excessively focused on the sexual aspect of clergy sexual misconduct, failing to see the wider picture—that this is only one way that power is being abused. In this reactive atmosphere we are in danger of pathologizing all sexual activity, forgetting that the sexual part of ourselves is a great gift to be celebrated and used with joy and wonder in our most intimate and committed relationships.

3. How open or closed is the congregation?

Organizations that become progressively closed to outside influences mirror many of the dynamics of incestuous families. People often do get sexually involved with each other in these settings. Often the only way a clergyperson can escape an excessively closed congregation is to burn out, act out, or leave prematurely. Conversely, a congregation with a long-tenured leader can become progressively more closed. Usually this happens gradually over many years. Then it can either explode (with a major trust betrayal) or implode, with everyone becoming collectively depressed.

4. What is the history of the congregation relative to other incidences of clergy burnout, such as serious illness, premature deaths, substance abuse, or other involuntary terminations not connected with betrayals of trust?

When a significant number of clergy over the years have somehow burnt out, an examination of why that has happened is imperative. Overwork and overfunctioning on the part of clergy can be a sign of an enormous amount of anxiety, either rooted in the congregation, or in families of key members or in the clergy families. Frequently these arenas overlap and the anxiety can get bounced back and forth, from one part of the system to another. Other situations that can contribute to the rise of anxiety levels are an aging, dying congregation, questions about viability of the congregation, serious unemployment in the community, and the need to face other major changes.

5. What is the congregation's entire history?

Often written or oral congregational histories can be gold mines of information. I emphasize here that we are not just looking for pieces of pathology. There will be inspiring events and strong clerical and lay leadership over the years that can be held up and celebrated. It can be tremendously helpful to study an earlier time when there was a "rough patch" and see what strengths the congregation called on to recover. The history of a congregation as a community of faith can be compared with other stories from Scripture and elsewhere. It is often possible to find metaphorical stories that speak to the deeper issues. By exploring the past, it is possible to better understand the present and look to the future with hope. Doing the work of visioning will go much better if the backwards look is taken first.

6. Are the expectations that congregants and clergy have of each other realistic?

Even in the healthiest of congregations expectations are often not realistic. In traumatized settings the expectations, often unspoken, can be real land mines. This is most likely to affect the relationship that clergy who follow the traumatic event, called "afterpastors," have with a congregation. Afterpastors frequently receive a lot of displaced anger, especially if that has not surfaced and been addressed during the recovery period.

7. What might it mean to truly embark on a mutual ministry that uses the strengths of laity in an intentional way?

Because a trust-betrayal event is so disempowering, looking for ways to empower the laity can be a significant corrective. This could be approached in both educational and symbolic ways. Many denominations offer special ministry training for laity. Symbolically, adult laity can be given more of a presence in the liturgy. People could also explore together their ingrained attitudes toward clergy and bring to the surface many of their unspoken beliefs. Raising to consciousness the ways people look to clergy to embody the divine could have the effect of demystifying and humanizing the clerical role. Clergy themselves will sometimes resist the idea of the empowerment of the laity. If they understand that empowerment will in the long run help make the church a safer place for everyone, they might be expected to be enthusiastic participants.

8. What do boundaries encompass in the broadest sense? How rigid or flexible should everyone's (not just clergy's) boundaries be in the congregation?

Many denominations have recently provided their clergy with seminars on healthy boundaries. This usually includes not just a narrow exploration of sexual boundaries but a look at the way the household and family of clergy interface with the congregation, and a very broad look at wellness issues. Because overwork is such an occupational hazard and the job itself is relatively boundary-less, many clergy need assistance in managing their time. Some will be examining their motives for overwork. Occasionally a clergyperson can be underfunctioning instead of overfunctioning. Two common reasons for this are that there is not enough work to be challenging or the person is depressed, sometimes keeping a frantic pace, then crashing and doing nothing. Clergy also need to be given permission to take time for themselves. But the maintenance of healthy boundaries for everyone in the congregation, not just the clergy, is a matter for the entire congregation to be aware of and to be working on together.

CONCLUSION

The Chinese character for crisis combines the two characters for "danger" and "opportunity." This is a good thing to keep in mind while navigating the choppy waters in the aftermath of a cleric's betrayal of trust. There certainly is danger, much of which has been addressed in this booklet. But there is also great opportunity. A crisis can have the effect of breaking open a congregation. There is a difference between breaking open and breaking apart. If people will work hard to respectfully listen to one another, to avoid laying blame, to stay the course and to work through the pain together, a much stronger congregation can emerge. This does take time, however. It takes the willingness to give others space to follow their own timetables and their own inner convictions. Spiritual renewal can come as people place their trust where it really belongs, in God.

About the Author:

Nancy Myer Hopkins is a licensed professional counselor who is a member of the board of the Interfaith Sexual Trauma Institute, Collegeville, Minnesota. She works nationwide as a consultant to churches and communities that have experienced betrayals of trust.